WHO DID IT FIRST?

50 POLITICIANS, ACTIVISTS, AND ENTREPRENEURS
WHO REVOLUTIONIZED THE WORLD

Henry Holt and Company, *Publishers since 1866*
Henry Holt® is a registered trademark of Macmillan Publishing Group, LLC
120 Broadway, New York, NY 10271 · mackids.com

Library of Congress Cataloging-in-Publication Data is available.
ISBN 978-1-250-21172-9

Our books may be purchased in bulk for promotional, educational, or business use.
Please contact your local bookseller or the Macmillan Corporate and Premium Sales Department
at (800) 221-7945 ext. 5442 or by email at MacmillanSpecialMarkets@macmillan.com.

First edition, 2020 / Designed by Carol Ly
Printed in China by 1010 Printing International Limited, North Point, Hong Kong
1 3 5 7 9 10 8 6 4 2

WHO DID IT FIRST?

50 POLITICIANS, ACTIVISTS, AND ENTREPRENEURS
WHO REVOLUTIONIZED THE WORLD

EDITED BY
ALEX HART

WRITTEN BY
JAY LESLIE

ILLUSTRATED BY
NNEKA MYERS

HENRY HOLT AND COMPANY · NEW YORK

CONTENTS

INTRODUCTION

The grandson of a slave was sworn in as the first African American Supreme Court justice. A young woman in exile rose to become Pakistan's first female prime minister. A girl so poor she wore potato sacks to school became the first African American female billionaire.

Thurgood Marshall, Benazir Bhutto, and Oprah Winfrey were pioneers. They beat the odds, overcoming prejudice and adversity to make history—and they're not the only ones.

In this book, you will find fifty inspirational leaders: politicians and athletes, activists and social entrepreneurs—people who changed the world by being the first in their fields. You'll learn how they overcame enormous challenges to achieve their dreams and make their communities a better place.

You might have an incredible, impossible dream. Maybe you dream of being the first Asian American class president of your school. Maybe you want to be the first woman elected the mayor of your town. Or maybe you aspire to be the first immigrant from your country to lead one of the largest companies in the United States. No matter the dream, regardless of scope, despite the odds . . . guess what: There's no such thing as impossible. Work hard. Stay focused. You *can* make your dream come true.

When you chase after your dreams, you make it possible for other people to achieve theirs too. Sirimavo Bandaranaike, who was elected the first female prime minister in the world in 1960, paved the way for Benazir Bhutto to lead Pakistan. The civil rights work that Thurgood Marshall began in 1934 influenced civil rights lawyer Barack Obama, who would go on to become the first African American president of the United States. Sarah Breedlove, who was recognized as the first American female self-made millionaire in the early 1900s, led the way for Oprah Winfrey.

As their stories inspire you, think about how your accomplishments will inspire someone else.

THOMAS GALLAUDET

THE FIRST PERSON TO ESTABLISH
A PERMANENT SCHOOL FOR THE DEAF
IN THE UNITED STATES (1817)

"

All the children OF SILENCE MUST BE TAUGHT TO SING their own song.

"

As a boy, Thomas excelled in his studies. He even graduated from Yale College when he was seventeen! But he didn't find his calling until he began tutoring Alice Cogswell, his neighbor's daughter, who couldn't hear or speak.

Many assumed that deaf children weren't smart enough to be formally educated. But Thomas realized that Alice could understand concepts as long as he explained them by writing them down. She *was* smart—she just needed more efficient ways to communicate. There were eighty-four other deaf people in Connecticut who needed a school. Thomas was asked to start one.

While trying to learn methods to educate the deaf, Thomas met Abbé Sicard, the head of a school for the deaf in France, who invited him to study the school's groundbreaking system: sign language. Thomas learned sign language quickly with the help of a deaf teacher, who then traveled around America with him, lecturing people about the importance of a school and trying to raise the funding to start it.

Thomas and his backers scraped together enough funds to found the American School for the Deaf in Hartford, Connecticut. It opened with seven students on April 15, 1817. They learned sign language in a flash, thrilled to be able to communicate more easily. By the end of the school's first year, enrollment had increased to thirty-three. Two years later, Congress granted the school a massive amount of land, the sale of which allowed it to buy property and build a permanent home.

In the past two hundred years, the American School for the Deaf has served more than six thousand students. Thomas's legacy also lives on in higher education. Gallaudet University is the only college in the world where all programs and services are designed for deaf and hard-of-hearing students.

SARAH WINNEMUCCA

THE FIRST NATIVE AMERICAN WOMAN
TO PUBLISH A BOOK (1883)

" I have worked for **FREEDOM.** I HAVE LABORED TO GIVE MY RACE **A VOICE** in the affairs of the nation. "

When Thocmetony, a Northern Paiute girl from Nevada, was thirteen, her parents sent her and her sister to live with a wealthy white family. The family insisted on calling her Sarah instead of Thocmetony. They also spoke to her in English instead of her native Paiute. No matter how much Sarah tried to fit in, she knew that she never would; the white family would never see Native Americans as equals.

In the 1860s, white settlers began stealing land that had been set aside for the Northern Paiute. Sarah returned from a trip to discover that the Nevada cavalry had raided a Paiute settlement and murdered twenty-nine people. Heartbroken, she dedicated herself to improving conditions for her people by building better relationships with the white settlers. But life got harder as land grabs continued and dishonest reservation agents withheld government food and supplies.

In 1878, a few Paiutes got caught up in a war between the Bannock people and the US government. As punishment, more than five hundred Paiutes were exiled 350 miles north to the Yakama Indian Reservation. Forced to cross two mountain ranges in the dead of winter, many of Sarah's people died. Starvation and disease killed so many more that the Yakama graveyard soon overflowed.

Sarah journeyed to Washington, DC, where she persuaded the secretary of the interior to allow the Northern Paiute to return to their homeland. He agreed—only to change his mind after she left. Undeterred, Sarah testified directly to Congress about the abuses she witnessed at Yakama, and she traveled across the states, delivering more than three hundred speeches about the mistreatment of her people. To reach an even wider audience, she compiled her speeches into an autobiography, *Life Among the Paiutes: Their Wrongs and Claims*. Although no Native American woman had ever published a book, two well-connected Boston sisters made it happen.

Sarah's book is still in print today, a testament to the bravery of a woman who dedicated her life to her people.

SUSAN LA FLESCHE

THE FIRST NATIVE AMERICAN WOMAN TO EARN A MEDICAL DEGREE IN THE UNITED STATES (1889)

My office hours are any and all hours of the day and night.

As a child, Susan La Flesche sat by a sick Omaha woman. A messenger went for the reservation doctor four times, but he never showed. As Susan watched the woman die, she decided to do whatever it took to give every member of her tribe proper health care.

Susan threw herself into her studies and enrolled at the Hampton Normal and Agricultural Institute in Virginia, where she graduated as salutatorian of her class. Her parents expected her to then return home and get married. But Susan applied to medical school.

Pursuing a medical degree as a woman, let alone a Native American woman, was almost impossible in 1886. First, Susan had trouble finding an institution that would admit her. Once she was accepted to the Woman's Medical College of Pennsylvania, she couldn't afford tuition. Susan appealed to the kindness of the Connecticut Indian Association. The association agreed to finance her training and solicited the residents of Connecticut to contribute. Susan thrived at the medical school in Philadelphia, but in her second year, an outbreak of measles swept through the Omaha Reservation, forcing her to return home. She was plagued by her own health problems, which would eventually leave her deaf. But Susan was determined; she finished her studies and graduated at the top of her class. She returned to the reservation, where she took care of 1,200 people across 450 square miles for twenty-five years. In 1913, two years before she died, she opened the Dr. Susan LaFlesche Picotte Memorial Hospital on the reservation, the first hospital built to serve the Omaha people.

SARAH BREEDLOVE

THE FIRST SELF-MADE FEMALE MILLIONAIRE IN THE UNITED STATES (1906)

"

DON'T SIT DOWN
and wait for
OPPORTUNITIES TO COME.
GET UP
and make them.

"

As the daughter of recently freed slaves and the first person in her family to be born free, Sarah Breedlove never took freedom for granted. She decided that the best way to take advantage of this freedom was to embrace the opportunities that her parents never had.

Even though she hadn't been a slave, life in America was still hard. She was forced to take a job as a laundress, toiling long hours for very little money. Unfortunately, no matter how much she scrimped and saved, she could hardly make ends meet, and the stress began to make her hair fall out. Thanks to infrequent washing and bad hygiene, many women were balding and suffering from dandruff, and all the stress they faced at their difficult jobs just made the problem worse.

With a burst of inspiration, Sarah realized that she could help thousands of women learn to love and care for their hair. Her brothers, who ran a barbershop, taught her everything they knew, and she learned the ins and outs of selling hair products by working under Annie Turnbo, an African American businesswoman and inventor. With their help, Sarah devised a special formula of hair products that would help heal women's damaged scalps. She started small, manufacturing her products by hand and selling them door-to-door, but after a few short years, her business had exploded so much that she needed to build a special house and a factory—and soon she added a hair salon, a beauty school, and even a laboratory! But Sarah didn't keep her hard-won business skills to herself; convinced that every black woman should be in charge of her own finances, she also taught classes on budgeting and entrepreneurship.

Sarah's products made her a millionaire, but the money wasn't her biggest accomplishment. In fact, she left most of her profits to charity. No, her biggest accomplishment was giving her daughter the resources and opportunities she and her parents had never had, and, in 1919, when Sarah passed away, her daughter confidently took over her mother's empire.

LIN ZONGSU

THE FIRST PERSON TO FOUND
A WOMEN'S SUFFRAGE ORGANIZATION IN CHINA (1911)

"

*As we enter a new century, women will leave
behind thousands of years of darkness.*

"

Lin Zongsu was no ordinary girl. Even as a child, she refused to conform, and preferred studying Russian revolutionary philosophy over traditional Chinese texts. Inspired by martyr and activist Qiu Jin, young Zongsu began to dream about a China where all citizens had equal rights.

At the turn of the twentieth century, she cofounded the first Chinese association for female students, the Mutual Love Society, and used it to advocate for every woman's right to an education. She later wrote about gender equality for her brother's newspaper, *Chinese Vernacular News*, as one of China's first female editors and journalists.

But Zongsu wasn't content to just write—she longed to fight on the front lines. So in 1911, she formed the Women's Suffrage Comrades' Alliance to protest for the right to vote, and she demanded an audience with China's president, Sun Yat-sen. Behind closed doors, Sun agreed that women should be able to vote and promised to make it happen. But when Zongsu published his agreement in the *Shenzhou Daily*, a political party important to Sun became outraged, and Sun backed out of his promise. Inspired by Zongsu, other women's rights groups rallied around the cause. Still, the president refused to include the clause in the 1912 constitution. Political uprisings beginning in 1913 effectively ended democracy for all people, men and women. To avoid being arrested, Zongsu had to go into hiding.

The Women's Suffrage Comrades' Alliance and Zongsu paved the way for the next generation of suffragists, and, in 1949, women finally received the right to vote in China.

GEORGE SHIMA

THE FIRST JAPANESE AMERICAN MILLIONAIRE (1913)

> " *If I can out-pick the Americans, I can also out-grow them.* "

Kinji Ushijima saw the silver lining in every cloud. After failing an exam to get into a top Japanese university, he decided to make a name for himself in America—literally. The industrious young man changed his name to George Shima and packed his bags.

In 1889, George arrived in San Francisco. Despite not knowing English, he resolved not only to become fluent but also to master the ins and outs of the American economy. He found employment as a house servant in order to rub elbows with wealthy Americans and, after a few months, entered a potato-picking contest to try his hand at agriculture. Although his white competitors cheated by stealing his potatoes, George won every single contest by a landslide! Realizing he had a knack for working the soil, he became a farmer.

Unfortunately, the only land he could afford was cheap swampland that no one else wanted. It was rancid with filthy water and infested with malaria-ridden mosquitoes. But George just rolled up his sleeves and set to work. He hired laborers to drain the swamp in a process called reclamation. George decided to plant rice, which was considered an emerging staple crop—but the crop failed. He'd invested all his money into this land and couldn't afford another bad harvest. He then remembered his potato-picking days. If he could get potatoes to grow in the swamp, he could sell them at a low price and make a fortune. It took him ten years to perfect his technique, but eventually his potatoes grew heavy and healthy, and everyone on the West Coast wanted a bite.

In 1913, George's potato empire earned enough profit to make him a millionaire. The newspapers crowned him the Potato King of California.

SIRIMAVO BANDARANAIKE

THE FIRST FEMALE PRIME MINISTER IN THE WORLD (1960)

Sirimavo Bandaranaike was born into one of the most distinguished families in Sri Lanka. Her ancestors were courtiers to Sinhalese rulers. She could trace her heritage back to a powerful monarchy, and she was expected to behave befitting her family's good name.

But she didn't care about any of that.

What Sirimavo *did* care about was people: Rich, poor, educated, uneducated, it didn't matter. She had a heart for everyone in Sri Lanka. She threw herself into social work, organized clinics, and worked on behalf of the rural poor. During a malaria epidemic in 1934–1935, she rolled up her sleeves and distributed food and medicine wherever it was needed.

In those days, women lacked the same political power as men, and Sirimavo decided to work with her husband instead of on her own. After she persuaded him to resign from the ruling party, he started his own political party to better focus on the needs of the poor. Citizens rallied to his message, electing his coalition into power, and Bandaranaike became prime minister in 1956. But after three years, he was assassinated. Realizing that no politician could understand her husband's work as deeply as she did, she stepped up to lead his party. She campaigned for the fair, equal society that they had envisioned for Sri Lanka. Her love for her people shone through, and in 1960, Sirimavo became the world's first female prime minister.

Her work paved the way for every female politician who came after her: Indira Gandhi, Margaret Thatcher, Benazir Bhutto, Angela Merkel, Ellen Johnson Sirleaf—and many more.

HISTORY

"

is full of examples of the

DISASTROUS

CONSEQUENCES

THAT CAME UPON SUCH NATIONS

that changed their constitutions by

GIVING ONE MAN

TOO MUCH POWER.

"

—SIRIMAVO BANDARANAIKE

TURN THE PAGE TO MEET SOME MORE

WOMEN WHO RULED

ELISABETH DOMITIEN
CENTRAL AFRICAN REPUBLIC (1975)

MARÍA CORAZON AQUINO
THE PHILIPPINES (1986)

Ertha Pascal-Trouillot
HAITI (1990)

ÉDITH CRESSON
FRANCE (1991)

YINGLUCK SHINAWATRA

THAILAND (2011)

LUCINA DA COSTA GOMEZ-MATHEEUWS

NETHERLANDS ANTILLES (1977)

JÓHANNA SIGURÐARDÓTTIR

ICELAND (2009)

Roza Otunbayeva

KYRGYZSTAN (2010)

WOMEN WHO RULED

 **ELISABETH DOMITIEN** (1925–2005) was prime minister of the Central African Republic from January 1975 to April 1976, making her Africa's first female prime minister and the first black woman ruler of an independent state. She fought for her country's liberation, the voice of the people, and the position of women.

 **LUCINA DA COSTA GOMEZ-MATHEEUWS** (1929–2017) was the first female prime minister of the former Netherlands Antilles (located off the coast of Venezuela). She held the office briefly in 1977. Prior to that, she was minister of health and environment, welfare, youth, sports, culture, and recreation.

 **MARÍA CORAZON AQUINO** (1933–2009) served as president of the Philippines from 1986 to 1992 and was the first woman to hold the title. She restored democratic rule to the country after a long period of dictatorship under Ferdinand Marcos (who had María's husband assassinated). The year she was elected, she was named *Time* magazine's Woman of the Year.

 **ERTHA PASCAL-TROUILLOT** (born 1943) was the first woman to hold the office of president in Haiti, from 1990 to 1991. Prior to that, she was a justice on the Haitian Supreme Court (again, the first woman to hold the position) and a judge in the federal court of Haiti. She has nine siblings.

 **ÉDITH CRESSON** (born 1934) is the only woman to have been prime minister of France. She held the role briefly, from May 1991 to April 1992, resigning after public support of her dwindled. Édith was also the first female agriculture minister in France. Today, she is a member of the Council of World Women Leaders.

 **JÓHANNA SIGURÐARDÓTTIR** (born 1942) became Iceland's first female prime minister in February 2009, a position she occupied until May 2013. She was also the world's first openly lesbian head of government. As a direct result of her governance, Iceland became a model for gender equality.

 ROZA OTUNBAYEVA (born 1950) served from 2010 to 2011 as the first female president of Kyrgyzstan, a country in central Asia that was once part of the Soviet Union. A former philosophy professor, she stepped down after losing the 2011 presidential election, displaying the country's first peaceful transfer of power.

YINGLUCK SHINAWATRA (born 1967) became the twenty-eighth—and first female—prime minister of Thailand in 2011. She was removed from office by the Constitutional Court of Thailand, which found her guilty of charges of abuse, in 2014. She fled Thailand in 2017.

As of 2020, more than 100 countries (there are currently 195 countries in the world) have never elected or appointed a woman to the top leadership position. They include Spain, Japan, Russia, and the United States.

ED ROBERTS

THE FIRST PERSON WITH QUADRIPLEGIA
TO ATTEND UC BERKELEY (1962)

"

If we have learned **ONE THING FROM THE** CIVIL RIGHTS MOVEMENT IN THE UNITED STATES *it's that when others* SPEAK FOR YOU, YOU LOSE.

"

For his first thirteen years, Ed Roberts was just like other boys. But at fourteen, he contracted polio—a disease that left him with quadriplegia—and was paralyzed from the neck down. Ed transformed from a boy who could run, jump, and play into a young man who could only move his head and two fingers.

Ed had to sleep in an eight-hundred-pound iron lung to breathe at night, and he attended high school over the phone from his bedroom. But he needed to get out of the house, so he returned to the classroom for his senior year. Classmates gawked. Ed wanted to hide, but he decided that they were staring in fascination, as if he were a celebrity. That gave him the confidence that he needed to graduate. However, the principal said he couldn't. Ed had not taken gym class or driver's ed! Ed and his mother had to fight to get the requirement waived before Ed received his diploma.

Ed next set his sights on college. He was excited to begin his first year at the University of California, Berkeley. The university was hesitant: Despite his good grades, the campus wasn't accessible; there were too many issues. (One of the deans even told him, "We've tried cripples before and it didn't work.") But Ed didn't back down. His iron lung was a big issue. The dorm floors couldn't support the weight. He was offered a room in the hospital, and Ed agreed, as long as he was not treated like a patient. He hired his own attendants and navigated the inaccessible campus. Seeing his success, the university admitted other students with severe disabilities and housed them in the same wing.

In 1964, Ed graduated from Berkeley with his bachelor's degree in political science. He returned for his master's, studied for his doctorate, and, eventually, taught there, focusing on disability rights activism. In 1972, he helped found the Center for Independent Living in Berkeley, a groundbreaking initiative that enabled people with disabilities to be self-sufficient.

Thanks to Ed, students with disabilities have been empowered to fight for the resources they deserve.

KATHARINE GRAHAM

THE FIRST FEMALE PRESIDENT OF THE *WASHINGTON POST* (1963)

"

*Left alone, no matter at what age or under
what circumstance, you have to remake your life.*

"

Katharine Graham was born into a wealthy family that valued propriety above all; she was expected to behave a certain way in society. Her parents never paid much attention to her, and she lived in the shadow of her elder siblings.

Despite her complicated relationship with her parents, Katharine followed in their footsteps and pursued a career in journalism. Her father bought the *Washington Post* when it went bankrupt, and her mother wrote for the paper. Katharine wrote for a paper in San Francisco before joining the *Post*. Still, when her father retired, he passed control of the newspaper to Katharine's husband instead of her.

Tragedy struck when her husband died suddenly in 1963. Katharine had no time to grieve because greedy media moguls circled the *Post*, plotting to take it over. If Katharine wanted the *Post* to remain in her family, she would have to run it herself. Overwhelmed, she agreed to lead the paper until her son was old enough to take control. But no one expected what happened next: Katharine became a strong, fearless leader. The *Post* ran world-changing stories—about the Pentagon Papers, top-secret documents about the Vietnam War; and Watergate, the scandal that brought President Nixon's shady dealings to light. The *Post* earned great acclaim and success.

Katharine wrote a memoir of her life's journey in journalism, *Personal History*. It won a Pulitzer Prize in 1998.

PATSY MINK

THE FIRST WOMAN OF COLOR ELECTED
TO THE UNITED STATES CONGRESS (1964)

Growing up as a third-generation Japanese immigrant in Hawaii, Patsy Mink witnessed racism firsthand. After seeing her father mistreated at his job, she devoted herself to ending discrimination.

This seemed impossible. After graduating from the University of Hawaii, she planned to attend medical school. All twenty schools that she applied to turned her down—she suspected it was because they refused to accept a woman. Outraged, she enrolled in law school to learn how to combat sexism. But once she graduated, she faced similar discrimination—no firms wanted to hire an Asian American woman. Discouraged but not defeated, she decided to partner with her husband and open her own law firm instead. She became the first Japanese American woman to practice law in Hawaii.

When Hawaii became a state in 1959, Patsy leaped at the opportunity to make a difference, so she campaigned for the US House of Representatives. But because she was an outspoken woman of color who didn't always agree with the white male Democrats in her party, many Democrats opposed her campaign—some even organized deals to help a Republican win instead of her! Without their help, Patsy funded her campaign herself and organized it from the ground up, supported by unpaid volunteers who worked tirelessly. It took her five long years, but she finally won a seat in the House in 1964.

In office, Patsy championed women's and minorities' rights. She is best known as one of the authors of Title IX, a bill that bars sexual discrimination in education or any other activity that receives federal funding. Today, thanks in large part to Patsy, women can attend the same schools that she was barred from.

"

It is easy enough
TO VOTE RIGHT
and be consistently with
THE MAJORITY ...
but it is often more important to
BE AHEAD
OF THE MAJORITY,

AND THIS MEANS
BEING WILLING
to cut the first
FURROW
IN THE GROUND AND
STAND ALONE
for a while if necessary.

99

—PATSY MINK

INDIRA GANDHI

THE FIRST FEMALE PRIME MINISTER OF INDIA (1966)

"

The power to question is the basis of all human progress.

"

As a child, Indira Gandhi frequently felt insecure. Her bedridden mother was too sick to take care of her, and her father, Jawaharlal Nehru, was often imprisoned as he worked for India's freedom from British colonialism.

At age twelve, Indira supported India's fight for freedom by leading the Vanar Sena—the Monkey Brigade. This coalition of 60,000 children made flags, relayed messages, and circulated announcements about political demonstrations. They were young, but they played their part.

Her father became India's first prime minister in 1947, and Indira worked as his personal assistant and hostess, taking an active role in the ruling political party, the Indian National Congress. The party elected her to a one-year term as its president in 1959. When her father died in 1964, she became minister of information and broadcasting for the new prime minister, Lal Bahadur Shastri. India's mostly male Congress hatched a scheme. Because she was a woman, they assumed that she would be submissive and easy to control, so they decided to elect her prime minister. Political leaders all across the country liked this plan, conspiring to use her as a puppet. One prominent opponent even called Indira their *goongi gudiya*—a "mute doll." But the would-be puppeteers were in for a rude awakening. Once Indira got into office, she ruled with her own sense of social justice for sixteen years. She helped Bangladesh achieve political and religious independence, and she improved international trade.

India has not had another female prime minister. But perhaps there is a girl out there right now who, like her, is quietly waiting for her turn before she steps up to lead the government with an iron will.

THURGOOD MARSHALL

THE FIRST AFRICAN AMERICAN SUPREME COURT JUSTICE (1967)

"

You do what you think is right and let the law catch up.

"

As the grandson of a slave, Thurgood Marshall did not have greatness handed to him on a silver platter. He struggled to get a good education in the segregated public-school system and was rejected by his top-choice law school because of his race. Defeated, he settled on a historically black institution instead.

Due to lack of funds and resources, predominantly black schools rarely offered the same caliber of education. After he became a lawyer and was working for the NAACP, Thurgood argued this fact vehemently in front of the US Supreme Court in the 1952 case *Brown v. Board of Education of Topeka*. The court agreed with him; finally, after nearly sixty years, they abolished the "separate but equal" segregation policy. As a fiery lawyer, Thurgood argued thirty-one more cases in front of the Supreme Court, fighting

for civil rights and gender equality and opposing police brutality and the death penalty.

Unfortunately, many people disliked the progressive changes that Thurgood stood for. When President Johnson nominated him to the Supreme Court, many segregationists in Congress bristled at the idea of a black man on the bench, so they did everything in their power to block his appointment. At his confirmation hearing, they grilled him longer than any Supreme Court nominee had ever been questioned before. But Thurgood remained calm. The senators voted him in on August 30, 1967.

Thurgood served on the Supreme Court for twenty-four years. When he stepped down in 1991, another African American justice named Clarence Thomas took his place and is still serving today.

YVON CHOUINARD

THE FIRST PERSON TO FOUND A MAJOR CLOTHING COMPANY THAT FOCUSES ON ENVIRONMENTAL ACTIVISM (1970)

"
How you climb a mountain is more important than reaching the top.
"

When he was seven, Yvon Chouinard moved to California, where he explored the ocean, creeks, and valleys. He fell in love with nature and decided he would do anything he could to protect it.

Unable to afford expensive climbing gear, he bought an anvil and forge and taught himself blacksmithing. He fashioned his own spikes, or pitons, out of metal he salvaged. Soon other climbers wanted his pitons, and he began selling them out of his car. Demand grew so much that he partnered with a fellow climber to produce climbing gear on machines. In 1970, he returned from a trip to Scotland with a brightly colored rugby shirt that had kept him warm on long climbs, and soon he was selling those too. Within a few years, his pitons and his shirts blossomed into full businesses. He named his equipment company Chouinard Equipment and his clothing company Patagonia.

Unfortunately, Yvon's businesses began destroying the very environment that he loved. So Yvon developed a new type of environmentally friendly climbing tools. In the 1990s, Patagonia commissioned a study on four major fibers used in clothing, which discovered that the natural fiber, cotton, had the worst environmental impact. The pesticides used to grow cotton pollute soil and water and potentially harm field workers. So he switched to organic cotton.

Time after time, Yvon demonstrated the importance of accountability; whenever he realized that one of his products was harming the environment, he sprang into action to right the wrong. To this day, as Chouinard Equipment and Patagonia thrive, Yvon is still doing what he loves: spending time in nature.

SALLY PRIESAND

THE FIRST FEMALE RABBI IN THE UNITED STATES (1972)

> *"*
>
> *I have always tried, after opening the door,
> to keep the door open for others to follow me.*
>
> *"*

Although her parents didn't raise her to be religious, Sally Priesand always felt connected to God. When she was sixteen, she decided that she was going to become a rabbi. The only problem? The United States had never had a female rabbi before.

She inquired about applying to a program that allowed students to complete the first year of rabbinical school while still in college. The Hebrew Union College–Jewish Institute of Religion was less than enthusiastic. "The question of a woman as a rabbi is a question for the rabbis rather than for the School," the school responded. "There is no attempt on our part to discourage you but to direct your thinking." (Rabbis had answered the question thirty years earlier when Regina Jonas was ordained as the first female rabbi in the 3,800-year history of Judaism.) But Sally didn't give up. She was accepted into the program as a "special student," enrolled "for credit but not as a Pre-Rabbinic student."

As an undergraduate, Sally got to know the faculty, and she was accepted as a rabbinical student after graduation. She had thirty-five classmates—all men. The rabbis who trained her didn't think that she would last long, and her classmates suspected she was only there to find a husband. Sally felt she had to be better than her classmates, so she studied harder. She was ordained June 3, 1972. As she was called to the bimah, all her classmates spontaneously stood up to salute her.

In 2012, the rabbinical school invited Sally back to the ordination ceremony as an honored guest. Thirteen rabbis were ordained that year; eight of them were women. Thanks to Sally, more than three hundred women have become rabbis in America.

MUHAMMAD YUNUS

THE FIRST PERSON TO PIONEER MICROFINANCE ON A MASSIVE SCALE (1976) AND THE FIRST BANGLADESHI TO JOINTLY WIN A NOBEL PEACE PRIZE (2006)

"

THERE ARE TWO KINDS OF

BUSINESSES

IN THE WORLD.

One is a business

WHICH MAKES MONEY,

AND THE OTHER SOLVES

the problems

OF THE WORLD.

"

The smallest things can sometimes make the biggest impact. Economist Muhammad Yunus learned this in 1976, when he visited rural Jobra, among the poorest villages in Bangladesh.

The women there supported themselves by selling handcrafted bamboo furniture. But they struggled to make ends meet because banks refused to loan them money to buy supplies—the banks considered them risky investments—so the women had to borrow from loan sharks who charged very high interest. Muhammad realized that these entrepreneurs just needed small amounts of money (called microloans) in order to lift themselves out of poverty. He opened his wallet and lent $27, which is the equivalent of $119 today, to the forty-two women in the village. They used it to successfully launch their businesses within a matter of months. A small amount of money changed their lives and showed them that they had the power to control their own finances, their own businesses, and their own futures.

Inspired, Muhammad founded Grameen Bank (*grameen* means "village") to give microloans to industrious people like these women. Not everyone was excited to see Grameen Bank succeed; fearing female independence, some conservative clergymen forbade women from taking any money. But by May 2008, the bank had made small loans totaling $7 billion to help 7.5 million people rise out of poverty. Ninety-seven percent of these loans went to women, who are often locked out of economies in developing countries. One hundred countries have followed in Grameen's footsteps by opening similar banks.

In 2006, Muhammad became the first Bangladeshi to receive a Nobel Peace Prize. He accepted the award with a smile and announced his plans: He'd use part of the prize money to develop cheap but nutritious food for the poor, and the rest to establish an eye hospital in Bangladesh, also for the poor. For more than forty years, Muhammad has never stopped advocating for those in need.

SANDRA DAY O'CONNOR

THE FIRST FEMALE SUPREME COURT JUSTICE (1981)

> "
> *The power I exert on the court depends on the power of my arguments, not on my gender.*
> "

As a child in Arizona, Sandra Day O'Connor shot jackrabbits and mastered driving when she was tall enough to see over the steering wheel. From a young age, she knew that if anything was going to get done, she would have to do it herself.

Sandra went on to college and then law school at Stanford. Even though she worked hard, she was a woman at a time when most law firms were hesitant to hire women. When no private firm would hire her, she turned to the public sector. Her government work continued as she handled contracts for the US military in Germany. Back in Arizona, Sandra started her own law practice, worked as an assistant attorney general, and then served five years in the state senate. In 1974, she became a judge.

In 1981, President Ronald Reagan chose her to be the first woman to serve on the US Supreme Court. Although Reagan was a conservative Republican himself, many conservatives opposed the nomination. They distrusted her position on women's reproductive rights and blasted her support of the Equal Rights Amendment. She underwent a grueling confirmation hearing that lasted for three days. The Senate finally confirmed her with a vote of 99 to 0. On September 25, 1981, she was sworn in as the first female Supreme Court justice of the United States.

Sandra paved the way for other women. Today, her legacy lives on through Justice Ruth Bader Ginsberg, Justice Sonia Sotomayor, and Justice Elena Kagan.

STEVE JOBS

THE FIRST PERSON TO INTRODUCE A
MASS MARKET PERSONAL COMPUTER WITH A
GRAPHICAL INTERFACE AND MOUSE (1984)

"

THE ONLY WAY TO BE
TRULY SATISFIED
IS TO DO WHAT YOU BELIEVE IS GREAT WORK.

And the only way to
DO GREAT WORK IS
TO LOVE
what you do.

"

As a child, Steve Jobs brought chaos wherever he went. He acted out in class, hated authority figures, and constantly played pranks. He was such a terrible toddler that his mother regretted adopting him, and later admitted, "I wanted to return him."

But underneath all of that trouble was an insatiable curiosity and a brilliant mind. He attended Reed College briefly but dropped out because he couldn't see the value in spending all his parents' money when he didn't even know what he wanted to do with his life. Still, he would sneak into classes just to listen. There, a calligraphy course changed his life by opening his mind to the importance of design.

He began to think hard about how he could merge his creative passions with his love of computers. After he returned from an inspiring trip to India, he teamed with his friend Steve Wozniak, who had come up with a new circuit board for a microcomputer. They founded a tiny company in 1976 called Apple to sell the circuit boards. Steve soon realized a complete computer, with a color monitor housed in a sleek plastic case, would appeal to the average person. Steve and Woz introduced Apple II in 1977 and sales took off.

Apple grew steadily but faced increasing competition from IBM. So in 1984, Steve unveiled a bold new idea. Back then, icons didn't exist and users couldn't click a button to start a program; they had to type commands with their keyboards. Jobs wanted to change that. He unveiled the Macintosh, an inexpensive computer with a graphical user interface built around icons. Users could now easily navigate their computers with a mouse. He used his knowledge of design to make the sleekest computer the world had ever seen. Today, nearly every computer uses a graphical user interface, and Macintoshes are still some of the most popular desktops and laptops in the world.

Even after he transformed the face of technology with the Mac, Steve didn't stop innovating. In 2001, he revolutionized the world with the iPod and then again with the iPhone in 2007.

BENAZIR BHUTTO

THE FIRST WOMAN TO SERVE AS PRIME MINISTER OF PAKISTAN (1988)

> *[A] whole series of people opposed me simply on the grounds that I was a woman.*

A great leader makes great sacrifices. As the daughter of the prime minister of Pakistan, Benazir Bhutto learned this lesson when the military overthrew her father's government and demanded that he be tried and eventually executed.

To keep Benazir from working on her father's behalf, military leaders detained her six times over a two-year period, sentenced her to house arrest for six months, and then locked her in jail for three years before exiling her to Europe. Although Benazir initially wanted to "be a diplomat, perhaps do some journalism," the hardship inspired her to try to fulfill her father's vision for a progressive Pakistan. When she returned in 1986, she announced her plan to run for prime minister, which enraged Muslim leaders—no Muslim country had ever permitted a female ruler before.

Ignoring the voices that promised she would fail, Benazir focused on reaching everyday people. Using her father's slogan, she would champion *"roti, kapra aur makan"* (bread, clothes, and housing) for all as well as free education and much-needed health care. Voters swarmed to support her, and on December 2, 1988, Benazir became the first female prime minister of Pakistan, the first female prime minister of a Muslim-majority country, and the Islamic world's youngest elected leader.

Benazir served two terms as prime minister. She eventually went into exile again. When allowed back in 2007, she announced plans to run for office. Three months later, she was assassinated by religious extremists.

JOAN GANZ COONEY

THE FIRST FEMALE NONPERFORMER TO BE INDUCTED INTO THE ACADEMY OF TELEVISION ARTS AND SCIENCES HALL OF FAME (1989)

> "
> *Our most precious resource in this country is our children, and they watch a lot of television.*
> "

Joan Ganz Cooney was born into a life of country clubs, where her parents expected her to marry by the time she turned twenty-five. Joan dreamed of becoming an actor, but her parents insisted that women should only be teachers—if anything at all.

But Joan wanted to make an impact beyond a single classroom. She produced documentaries about racial and economic inequality. When the films received many awards but few viewers, she brainstormed how to reach the age group that mattered the most: children. With the right TV show, she could provide a free, quality education to all preschoolers. After interviewing teachers, she envisioned a neighborhood full of quirky characters and bouncy music:

Sesame Street. This show could change the face of education!

Studio after studio disagreed, so she cofounded Children's Television Workshop and took production into her own hands. *Sesame Street* premiered on November 10, 1969. By 1979, 9 million children in the United States were watching it—per day! By 2006, the show was the most popular show in the world.

Although Joan never became an actor, she had a great impact. In 1989, the Academy of Television Arts and Sciences Hall of Fame inducted Joan as a member—they stood in awe of how groundbreaking *Sesame Street* was. And in 2007, she started The Joan Ganz Cooney Center, a nonprofit focused on improving children's learning through digital media.

ALTHEA GARRISON

THE FIRST TRANSGENDER LAWMAKER IN THE UNITED STATES (1993)

"
I believe there's a great opportunity for change.
"

Althea Garrison grew up as a black, transgender woman in the rural town of Hahira, Georgia. After high school, she moved to Boston to attend beauty school. A few years later, she decided to enter politics.

Her path to the state legislature was long and hard. She began her political career by running for the Massachusetts House of Representatives in 1982, determined to protect unions and ensure that all laborers were treated fairly. That year, she lost. She lost again in 1986. She ran for Boston City Council and lost five more times. But she refused to give up.

In 1992, she pursued the Massachusetts House of Representatives again. This time, she won! It was a victory, but not everyone saw it that way. Just days after she was elected, a *Boston Herald* reporter dug up her birth certificate, which stated that she was born male. The reporter cornered Althea and demanded to know if she was a man. She truthfully answered no. Unsatisfied, the *Herald* ran a story that revealed she was transgender and accused her of hiding her past. Some voters were outraged, but Althea held her head high, continued to serve, and ran for reelection in 1994. She lost. Undeterred, she ran many more times over the next twenty-three years, in elections for mayor, Boston City Council, and the Massachusetts legislature.

Her persistence finally paid off. She campaigned for the Boston City Council in 2017 and lost again. But nine months later, one of the at-large winners stepped down to run for Congress. By city rules the at-large seat went to the next-place finisher: Althea. She wasn't the only transgender woman to succeed in politics that election cycle; in November 2017 in Virginia, a journalist named Danica Roem became the first openly transgender person to be elected to a state legislature. Althea's determination helped make that possible.

NELSON MANDELA

THE FIRST BLACK HEAD OF STATE IN SOUTH AFRICA (1994)

Nelson Mandela was born into a bitterly divided South Africa in 1918. An oppressive system called apartheid denied black South Africans the right to vote, locked them out of high-paying jobs, and trapped them in a cycle of poverty. White South Africans, meanwhile, enjoyed access to education as well as the best jobs.

Outraged by the inequality, Nelson organized protests and led rallies with an activist group called the African National Congress. Terrified of his growing popularity, the government ordered him to stop speaking in public, but Nelson refused—the world needed to know about apartheid. So in 1964, after being caught planning a national revolution, he was sentenced to life in prison. Nelson continued to rail against injustices from behind bars, and he threw himself into legal studies, determined to understand the rights of his fellow citizens.

Thanks to international pressure, the South African government finally released Nelson in 1990, after twenty-seven long years. Instead of settling into a quiet life, the elderly Nelson immediately demanded that black South Africans be given the right to vote. The government reluctantly gave in, in time for the 1994 elections, and the country overwhelmingly elected Nelson's party, who chose him to be the head of state. This made him the first black person in South Africa to hold the position, effectively ending nearly fifty years of apartheid and segregation.

As he delivered his acceptance speech and looked out over the crowd, Nelson smiled, likely knowing that this was the beginning of a new era.

"

THE GREATEST GLORY *in living lies not in* NEVER FALLING,

BUT IN RISING *every time* WE FALL.

"

— NELSON MANDELA

KASHA NABAGESERA

THE FIRST PERSON TO FOUND A LESBIAN, BISEXUAL, AND TRANSGENDER RIGHTS ORGANIZATION IN UGANDA (2003)

> "
> *I may not live to see the freedom I am fighting for, but I am just happy to be part of the foundation for change.*
> "

As a child in Uganda, Kasha Nabagesera kept getting expelled from school. All she did was tell her classmates that she had a crush on them—why did it matter that those classmates were girls?

She hoped college would be better, but it wasn't. In her country, it was illegal to be who she was. Lesbian, gay, bisexual, and transgender people had no legal rights. She decided she needed to change that.

She and a group of gay women occasionally met to discuss this discrimination. In 2003, a tabloid outed them, and many were brutally attacked. Kasha decided to become an activist. She expanded the group into an official organization to defend the rights of lesbian, bisexual, and transgender people. Freedom and Roam Uganda was the first of its kind in the country. Through FARUG, she met with politicians, worked with organizations to make LGBT stories more positive, and led conferences around the country. Despite her hard work, lawmakers introduced a bill in 2009 that authorized the death penalty for repeatedly having same-sex relations. In 2010, a newspaper printed the names, photos, and addresses of a hundred gay Ugandans, with the label HANG THEM! But Kasha refused to give up.

In 2012, Uganda took a major leap forward: The very first health clinic for LGBT people opened in the capital city of Kampala. "It doesn't mean everything is OK," Kasha said, "but at least there's a very, very big difference from where we began."

SHIRIN EBADI

THE FIRST MUSLIM WOMAN TO RECEIVE A NOBEL PRIZE (2003)

"
It's not just about hope and ideas. It's about action.
"

Shirin Ebadi was born to a liberal family within a conservative country. Her parents treated her as an equal to her brothers. In fact, it wasn't until she was older that she realized most Iranian girls were considered second-class. The realization shocked her—and inspired her to take action.

Shirin threw herself into legal studies, even though law was thought to be a man's domain. But encouraged by her parents, Shirin ignored the naysayers and worked twice as hard. When she was only twenty-two, she became one of the first female judges in Iran's history! But she didn't stop there. She earned a doctorate at Tehran University in 1971, and in 1975 she was promoted to chief justice of Tehran's city court.

Everything changed after the country's Islamic Revolution in 1979, when a strict religious government came to power. The new regime believed Islam forbids women from serving as judges, so it immediately demoted Shirin to a secretary in the court she once presided over. Shirin quit. When she was finally allowed to practice law again, Shirin defended women and political dissidents and represented families of people killed in politically motivated attacks. This infuriated government officials, and they jailed her for a time.

Shirin continued to speak out about human rights, writing books and founding advocacy groups. In 2003, she was awarded the Nobel Peace Prize "for her efforts for democracy and human rights. She has focused especially on the struggle for the rights of women and children." She was the first Muslim woman ever to receive the honor.

In 2009, the Iranian government confiscated her medal and seized her bank accounts, accusing her of tax evasion. Shirin was forced into exile, but she hasn't stopped campaigning for the rights of women and children.

OPRAH WINFREY

THE FIRST AFRICAN AMERICAN FEMALE BILLIONAIRE (2003)

THE BIGGEST ADVENTURE *you can ever take is* TO LIVE THE LIFE OF *your dreams.*

— OPRAH WINFREY

The wealthiest African American woman in the United States began as one of the poorest. Oprah Winfrey was born in 1954 to an impoverished single mother in Mississippi. Her family was so poor that as a child Oprah wore dresses sewn from potato sacks. Her classmates laughed in her face and sneered behind her back; they called her "Sack Girl."

But Oprah had skill, and she sensed she was "destined for greatness." She boasted a thousand-watt smile and an easy laugh that made people feel comfortable around her. In high school, she debuted her speaking talents on the airwaves in Nashville, where she became the first black female news anchor in the city—and the station's youngest anchor up to that time. In 1984, she moved to Chicago to host a talk show struggling with low ratings, but Oprah knew that she could turn it around. Within a year, she had her own national show, the first African American to do so. Unlike other hosts, she didn't gossip about celebrities; she recorded hard-hitting episodes on spirituality, social issues, and politics. Just one year later, it became the highest-rated talk show in America—no wonder it ran for twenty-five years, from 1986 to 2011!

Unsatisfied with being only a television personality, Oprah expanded her empire into a magazine and also became the first African American to own a large production studio. In 2003, Oprah officially became the first African American female billionaire. She decided to pay her wealth forward, and, in 2004, she became the first African American to rank among the top 50 most generous Americans. By 2012, she'd donated more than $400 million to education, including funding 400 scholarships to Morehouse College.

Today, that poor little girl from Mississippi, who once wore potato sack dresses and struggled to hold her head high, is worth nearly $3 billion.

ANGELA MERKEL

THE FIRST FEMALE CHANCELLOR OF GERMANY (2005)

> "
> *We are a country based on democracy,*
> *tolerance, and openness to the world.*
> "

Angela Merkel grew up in East Germany under a strict, communist Russian government that kept an eye on everything she did. A young Angela dreamed of the day when she would have the freedom to be whoever she wanted.

She didn't always dream of becoming a politician. In fact, she earned a doctorate in quantum chemistry. For three years, she worked as a researcher—until one bright day in 1989 when the Soviets left Germany and East Germans were finally allowed free speech. Angela decided to get involved with politics. She began fixing computers for a local political group, the Democratic Awakening. She had such a calm, methodical mind and persuasive way of speaking that the group's leaders soon promoted her to be their spokesperson.

Angela was a soft-spoken woman in a government packed with outspoken men. She was a young scientist whose opponents were seasoned politicians. Few men took her seriously; even her mentor, Chancellor Helmut Kohl, condescendingly called her *mein Mädchen*, or "my girl," even though she was a grown woman. But Angela had one thing they didn't: patience. She viewed politics as a slow game of chess. As her opponents took one another down, Angela observed quietly from the sidelines. In 2005, when her opponents had destroyed one another, Angela stepped into the spotlight and calmly showed the German people who she was: a clear-headed, rational leader who could govern the country in peace.

On November 22, 2005, Angela became Germany's first female chancellor, a position that she still holds to this day. She has never been an ordinary politician—and that's what makes her so fit to lead.

ELLEN JOHNSON SIRLEAF

THE FIRST FEMALE HEAD OF STATE IN AFRICA (2005)

> "
> *The size of your dreams must always exceed your current capacity to achieve them.*
> "

Leadership ran in Ellen Johnson Sirleaf's blood. Her grandfather served as a Gola chief in Liberia, and from a young age, Ellen had cultivated a strong sense of right and wrong—a sense that would get her in trouble.

Ellen refused to let anyone or anything stand in her way. During an early speech to the Liberian Chamber of Commerce, she turned heads—and made enemies—when she accused local businesses of mistreating citizens. When a military dictatorship took over Liberia, she worked as a finance minister for the new government, but she lost her job for protesting the military's brutal policies. The dictator imprisoned her twice and then threatened to execute her. When she refused to back down, he exiled her in 1985.

Ellen wasn't allowed to return to Liberia until 1997, after a brutal civil war. Seeing the pain in her country, she ran for president. Even though she lost, her campaign sent a message to the people—she envisioned a new Liberia built on freedom and fairness. The country fell back into civil war in 1999, but when peace came in 2003, Ellen ran for president again. She swore to eliminate corruption, unify the country, rebuild infrastructure, and, most importantly, bring peace. Voters called her the "Iron Lady." After a close election, she was elected Liberia's first female president in 2005.

In 2011, Ellen won the Nobel Peace Prize. As she received the award, she beamed out at the crowd—she had a lot of work to do, and this was only the beginning.

BARACK OBAMA

THE FIRST AFRICAN AMERICAN
PRESIDENT OF THE UNITED STATES (2009)

Barack Obama was a born outsider. His father was a Kenyan goat herder, his mother was a white woman from Kansas, his parents were an interracial couple, and Barack was born in Hawaii in 1961—no president had ever been born there. But being an outsider taught him empathy for all types of people, a trait that molded him into a great leader.

As a young man, Barack dedicated himself to helping other outsiders. He became a community organizer, calling on corporations and politicians to stop overlooking poor people in Chicago. Determined to give a voice to the voiceless, he studied civil rights at Harvard Law School and worked so hard that he became the first African American president of the *Harvard Law Review*. Studious young Barack graduated at the top of his class.

Barack entered politics in order to affect civil rights laws firsthand. In 2004, he ran for US Senator of Illinois, and he didn't just win—he won with the largest landslide in the state's history! People rallied to his passion for equality. Barack realized that he could help the whole country, but he was nervous. He knew that being president would be the hardest thing he had ever done; many Americans were deeply racist, especially against African Americans, and weren't afraid to show it. On top of that, the United States was tangled in two complicated foreign wars, and the economy was so bad that millions of people couldn't find jobs. But because Barack felt a duty to the American people, he ran for president in 2008 with one word: hope. He won.

America still has a long way to go before healing its racial scars, but Barack Obama's landmark election sent a clear message: Anyone who truly cares about his or her country can be president.

"

CHANGE

will not come

IF WE WAIT
FOR SOME
OTHER PERSON

or some other time.

WE ARE
the ones we've been
WAITING FOR.
WE ARE
the change
THAT WE SEEK.

,,

—BARACK OBAMA

URSULA BURNS

THE FIRST AFRICAN AMERICAN CEO OF
A FORTUNE 500 COMPANY (2009)

"
The best way to change it is to do it.
"

Ursula Burns was born in an impoverished New York housing project in 1958. Her mother told her, "This is where you're going to grow up, but this is not what defines you." Ursula took that to heart and resolved to move her family into a better situation.

Fresh out of college, Ursula became an intern at Xerox Corporation. Interns were the lowest-ranking people in the company, but that didn't stop her from speaking her mind. Ursula always promoted her own ideas, and soon, all of the company managers knew her name. They watched as she worked her way up from intern, to executive assistant to the vice president for global manufacturing, to president of business group operations.

In 2000, Ursula declared that she wanted to be CEO. But the board members felt that she wasn't always a team player and still had a lot to learn. Over the next nine years, she set her mind to the task of absorbing everything she could about leadership and humility. Finally, in 2009, she made history by becoming the first African American CEO of a Fortune 500 company (a company ranked as one of the largest five hundred corporations in the United States).

As CEO, Ursula realized that being a team player also meant leading the way for future generations. So in 2009, she stepped up to run the White House's National Science, Technology, Engineering, and Math (STEM) initiative, starting federal programs to help give all students equal access to science and technology education. Thanks to her work, children growing up in the same New York housing project that she did now have access to the resources that she wishes she'd had as a child.

TAWAKKOL KARMAN

THE FIRST ARAB WOMAN TO WIN A NOBEL PRIZE (2011)

Each morning, when Tawakkol Karman walked to school, she knew that she was lucky. Not every girl in Yemen was allowed to attend school. In fact, some were forced to marry while they were still children. Tawakkol vowed that one day, she'd ensure every woman and girl in Yemen could have the same opportunities that she did.

In 2005, after earning a graduate degree in political science, she founded a human rights organization called Women Journalists Without Chains. She and seven female journalists wrote tirelessly about gender rights and encouraged women to speak up about the difficulties they faced. This enraged the conservative government. Desperate to keep her quiet, government officials threatened to hurt her if she didn't shut down her organization. Undaunted, Tawakkol spoke up louder! In 2007, she published a report about the government's mistreatment of journalists, and she began leading weekly demonstrations in Tahrir Square, the main gathering place in Yemen's capital city.

The protests grew quickly. By 2011, thousands of Yemenis were flooding the square in a massive wave of outrage against the president's corruption—he was silencing journalists, stealing public funds, and ignoring his people. Police officers threw Tawakkol in prison and ordered her to stop the protests, but she refused. The president even threatened to kill her, but that didn't scare her. Once she was released, she organized a "Day of Rage": a fiery, intense protest commanding the president to step down so that the people could choose their own leader. She was arrested again, but the outcry only grew, and finally, in 2012, the president left office.

In 2011, Tawakkol received the Nobel Peace Prize for all of the work she'd done to empower Yemeni women. As she accepted it, she said, "I am so happy, and I give this award to all of the youth and all of the women across the Arab world, in Egypt, in Tunisia. We cannot build our country or any country in the world without peace."

"

NOW IS THE TIME FOR
women
TO STAND UP
and become active
WITHOUT NEEDING
to ask for permission or
ACCEPTANCE.

"

— TAWAKKOL KARMAN

TURN THE PAGE TO MEET OTHER

YOUNG ACTIVISTS

Melati and Isabel Wijsen

FIRST ACTIVISTS TO SUCCESSFULLY CAMPAIGN
FOR THE ELIMINATION OF PLASTIC BAGS IN BALI (2016)

SHAMMA BINT SUHAIL FARIS MAZRUI

FIRST MINISTER OF STATE
FOR YOUTH AFFAIRS IN THE
UNITED ARAB EMIRATES (2016)

JASILYN CHARGER

FIRST PERSON TO CAMP ON THE STANDING
ROCK SIOUX RESERVATION IN PROTEST
OF THE DAKOTA ACCESS PIPELINE (2016)

HALIMA ADEN

FIRST HIJAB-WEARING
FASHION MODEL TO WALK ON
INTERNATIONAL RUNWAYS (2017)

MARVIA MALIK

FIRST OPENLY
TRANSGENDER NEWSREADER
IN PAKISTAN (2018)

Yara Shahidi

FOUNDER OF EIGHTEEN X 18 (2018)

YOUNG ACTIVISTS

 JASILYN CHARGER is a Lakota Sioux activist. She cofounded a youth group called One Mind Youth Movement (OMYM) in 2015 to support teens on the Cheyenne River Reservation in South Dakota. The group later evolved into a political movement when she and some other OMYM members set up camp at the Standing Rock Sioux Reservation in April 2016 to protest the construction of the Dakota Access Pipeline. More than ten thousand people joined Jasilyn and OMYM's protest over the next few months.

 MELATI AND ISABEL WIJSEN are sisters and activists from the Indonesian island of Bali. In 2013, at just twelve and ten years old, Melati and Isabel founded Bye Bye Plastic Bags, a nonprofit and nongovernmental organization that focuses on ridding Bali of plastic bags. Since founding Bye Bye Plastic Bags, Melati and Isabel have traveled the world, recorded a TED Talk, visited the United Nations, and, most importantly, successfully petitioned in 2016 for Bali's local government to ban all plastic bags.

 SHAMMA BINT SUHAIL FARIS MAZRUI is an Emirati politician. She has a bachelor's degree in economics from New York University Abu Dhabi and a master's of public policy from the University of Oxford, and she was the United Arab Emirates's first Rhodes Scholar. In 2016, Prime Minister Mohammed bin Rashid Al Maktoum appointed Shamma the minister of state for youth affairs in the UAE. Shamma was only twenty-two when she was selected, making her the youngest government minister in the world.

HALIMA ADEN is a Somali American fashion model. Born in a refugee camp in Kenya, Halima's family immigrated to St. Cloud, Minnesota, when she was seven years old. In 2016, at the age of nineteen, she became the first contestant in the history of the Miss Minnesota USA Pageant to wear a hijab and burkini. Despite the fact that she did not win, Halima signed with IMG Models. She became the first hijab-wearing model to walk international runways and the first hijab-wearing model to appear on the cover of *Vogue* magazine.

 MARVIA MALIK is a Pakistani newscaster and media figure. In 2018, she became the first transgender newscaster to appear on Pakistani television. Before working with Kohenoor News, Marvia worked as a makeup artist to help fund her university studies. She has a degree in journalism from the University of the Punjab in Lahore, Punjab, Pakistan. "Our society treats transgender people shamefully, degrading them, denying them jobs, laughing at them, and taunting them," Marvia said. "I want to change that."

 YARA SHAHIDI is an African American Iranian actress, model, and activist. In January 2018, ahead of her eighteenth birthday, Yara collaborated with the social news website NowThis News and founded Eighteen × 18, a creative platform with the goal of encouraging young people to express themselves and vote. In Yara's view, every young person has a voice that deserves to be heard, both in their personal and political lives.

HABEN GIRMA

THE FIRST DEAFBLIND GRADUATE OF HARVARD LAW SCHOOL (2013)

"
Fear causes people to lose so much. Lose potential knowledge, lose potential friends. I wish people would stop living in fear and start asking questions so that they can learn.
"

Haben Girma always knew that she could do anything she wanted. Being deaf and blind never stopped her from dancing, skiing, biking, kayaking, or even rock climbing!

Creativity was key. For example, when she struggled to navigate the cafeteria at her college, she devised an easy solution: If the cafeteria manager emailed her the menu, she could plan her route in advance. Unfortunately, the manager brushed her off. But Haben didn't back down. She educated him about Title III of the American Disability Act, which requires every business to accommodate people with disabilities, and then worked with him to improve the cafeteria's conditions. Thanks to Haben, the facilities became more accessible for all students.

After graduating, Haben enrolled as Harvard Law School's first deafblind student.

She connected a Bluetooth keyboard to a device that displayed braille, so her classmates could talk to her by typing. She arranged to receive readings digitally so that the same device could turn them into braille. To learn how deafblind students were treated abroad, she traveled to China to meet with the principal of the Beijing School for the Blind, and she showed him how deafblind students can learn sign language by feeling the signer's hands. When she graduated in 2013, she left Harvard much better equipped for students with disabilities who came after her.

In 2013, the White House named Haben a Champion of Change. For her, education and law go hand in hand: "A lawyer's job is always [as] an educator," she said. "An educator who has the potential to file complaints if people refuse to learn."

JANET MOCK

THE FIRST TRANSGENDER WOMAN OF COLOR
TO PUBLISH A BEST-SELLING MEMOIR (2014)

> *I believe that telling our stories, first to ourselves and then to one another and the world, is a revolutionary act.*

When Janet was five years old, a neighbor dared her to run across a parking lot in a dress. She did—and loved it. As the fabric fluttered around her ankles, Janet, who'd been born biologically male, felt like herself for the first time.

No matter how masculine her body looked, she knew that she was actually a girl. Her life changed when she made a transgender friend. As Janet became more comfortable expressing herself, she started wearing women's clothing to school. Her classmates taunted her and the vice principal kept sending her home, but Janet loved how she looked. She began taking female hormones to make her body more feminine. By the time she went to college, she fully felt like herself.

When Janet became a successful magazine editor, she decided not to tell her coworkers that she was transgender. But the more successful she became, the more she began to feel a responsibility to tell her story. She sat down with a reporter, but she didn't like the way the article turned out—it didn't feel authentic. So she decided to write an entire book in her own words. It wasn't easy! She worked on it for years. She called the book *Redefining Realness: My Path to Womanhood, Identity, Love & So Much More*. It flew off the shelves.

To this day, the book continues to give readers hope. And Janet continues to make history: In 2018, she became the first transgender woman of color to write and direct a TV episode (for *Pose*). And in 2019, she landed a deal with Netflix, another first for an out transgender woman of color.

SCHUYLER BAILAR

THE FIRST OPENLY TRANSGENDER NCAA DIVISION 1 SWIMMER (2016)

"

I really just want to be visible so people know this is possible, that I exist—not 'I' as in Schuyler, but 'I' as in a trans athlete.

"

Schuyler Bailar was a boy. So why couldn't anyone see that? His entire life, Schuyler had been told that he was a girl, and outwardly he looked like one, but he knew he wasn't. To cope with the discomfort, he began to swim; swimming was the only time he felt at peace in his own skin.

He tried to fit in with his female classmates by growing out his hair and imitating their behavior. But he was miserable, which led to an eating disorder and mental health issues. He clung to swimming, and when he broke a national record, Harvard University recruited him to its women's swim team. But his mental health worsened. After high school, he made the difficult decision to spend four months in a rehabilitation clinic. It was there that he acknowledged that he

was a transgender man. Still, he worried that if he started taking hormones to transition from female to male, Harvard would kick him off the women's team. Was it worth it?

In the end, Schuyler had to be true to himself. He began taking testosterone shots to deepen his voice and grow facial hair, documenting his process on Instagram. When Harvard saw how committed he was, it offered him a spot on the men's swim team. It would be hard work—although Schuyler had been a breakout star on the women's team, he'd now have to struggle at the bottom of the men's team as he got used to his new body.

Thanks to Schuyler, countless transgender athletes will find a place in Division I sports.

MELINDA GATES

THE FIRST WOMAN TO GIVE MORE THAN $40 BILLION TO CHARITY (2017)

"

IF YOU ARE SUCCESSFUL,

IT IS BECAUSE *somewhere, sometime,* SOMEONE GAVE YOU A LIFE OR AN IDEA *that started you in the* RIGHT DIRECTION.

"

Elaine French, Melinda Gates's mother, was a stay-at-home mom with one major regret: She wished that she had gone to college. From the time Melinda was young, her mother told her that education was the most important thing in the world.

Taking her mother's words to heart, Melinda threw herself into her studies and soon fell in love with advanced mathematics and computers. Captivated by the power of technology, she majored in computer science and economics at Duke University and then lent her talents to one of the most promising companies in the world: Microsoft. By working hard, she quickly advanced from being a project manager to overseeing dozens of groundbreaking products, including the travel website Expedia and the encyclopedia Encarta. But Melinda wasn't satisfied. She was successful in her career, possessed multiple degrees, and had fulfilled her mother's dream, but she knew that she could do more.

She remembered the importance of education. So after she married entrepreneur Bill Gates in 1994, she started the charitable organization that would later be known as the Bill & Melinda Gates Foundation. First, she focused on giving computers to schools all over the United States, but soon she started thinking about improving education worldwide. She said, "Bill and I believe education is the great equalizer." She also added projects to improve global health and started the Gates Millennium Scholars Program to help disadvantaged students attend college for free.

In 2016, President Barack Obama awarded her the Presidential Medal of Freedom in honor of all the good work that she had done, and, by 2017, she had given away more than $40 billion to charity.

JACINDA ARDERN

THE FIRST ELECTED HEAD OF STATE TO TAKE MATERNITY LEAVE (2018)

> "
>
> *It is a woman's decision about when they choose to have children, and it should not predetermine whether or not they are given a job or have job opportunities.*
>
> "

When she was a child, Jacinda Ardern saw the women around her having to make a difficult choice: Should they pursue a career, or should they raise a family? Men never had to choose—they could have both! From the moment her independent aunt Marie introduced her to politics, Jacinda decided she would achieve everything that she wanted without ever compromising.

Jacinda held fast to this belief. Before working with social justice movements in Jordan, Algeria, Israel, and China, she had been one of few female policy advisors in London, where she spoke out against men who were abusing their power. Jacinda worked twice as hard as her male counterparts, and her efforts paid off in 2017 when she became the prime minister of New Zealand.

On January 19, 2018, Jacinda announced that she was pregnant. Across New Zealand, people wondered: Could she lead a country while raising a family? Would she have to step down from office? But Jacinda had no plans to resign. Instead, she explained that she would be taking six weeks of maternity leave. The deputy prime minister would serve as the acting prime minister. This was the best decision not only for herself and her baby but also for her country. Taking maternity leave set the precedent that all workers should have time to spend with their children.

On June 21, 2018, Jacinda gave birth to a baby girl named Neve Te Aroha Ardern Gayford. When Neve grows up, thanks to her mother's bravery, she and women like her will have the freedom to choose.

LEBRON JAMES

THE FIRST NBA STAR TO
OPEN A PUBLIC SCHOOL (2018)

"

You have to
BE ABLE TO
ACCEPT
FAILURE
TO GET BETTER.

"

LeBron James grew up poor in Akron, Ohio, where he struggled even to make it to school every day. Unable to find secure employment, his mother moved him from place to place, so much so that he became disinterested and missed eighty-three days of fourth grade alone. That was the year his mother realized that she couldn't give him the one thing he really needed: a steady home with a regular routine. She sent him to live with Frank Walker, a local coach, who taught ten-year-old LeBron how to dribble a basketball and shoot left-handed layups. He changed LeBron's life.

The young player was a natural. He blew past all his competition on the court and made headlines for his exceptional skills. After a dominating high school career, he was drafted straight into the National Basketball Association as the number one pick in 2003. There he would make history, becoming the only NBA player ever to record at least 30,000 points, 8,000 assists, and 8,000 rebounds. But as he got older, he began to think about the importance of the education that he had missed.

LeBron returned to Akron with a vision. He wanted to start the school that he wished he'd had when he was young. In 2011, he launched the I Promise initiative in Akron's public schools to provide the support and structure he so desperately needed as a child. Six years later that initiative grew into a proposal for an entire school. The I Promise School, a public institution that required students to dedicate themselves to learning, health, and excellence, focused on low-performing students who needed individualized attention and after-school help. Students would go to class until five o'clock and have a shorter summer break; LeBron wanted to teach the kids to be serious about learning.

On July 30, 2018, the I Promise School opened with its first 240 third- and fourth-grade students. By 2022, the school will serve students all the way from first through eighth grade. LeBron is going to change these students' lives with education—and that's a promise.

What will YOU BE THE FIRST TO DO?

WHO DID IT FIRST?
ACROSS TIME

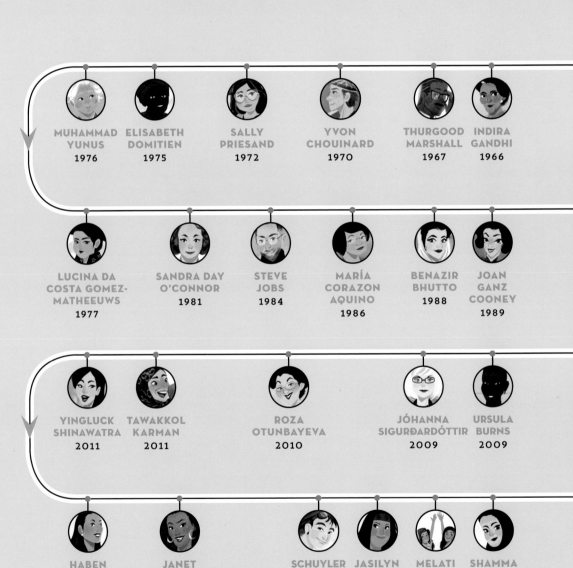

MUHAMMAD YUNUS
1976

ELISABETH DOMITIEN
1975

SALLY PRIESAND
1972

YVON CHOUINARD
1970

THURGOOD MARSHALL
1967

INDIRA GANDHI
1966

LUCINA DA COSTA GOMEZ-MATHEEUWS
1977

SANDRA DAY O'CONNOR
1981

STEVE JOBS
1984

MARÍA CORAZON AQUINO
1986

BENAZIR BHUTTO
1988

JOAN GANZ COONEY
1989

YINGLUCK SHINAWATRA
2011

TAWAKKOL KARMAN
2011

ROZA OTUNBAYEVA
2010

JÓHANNA SIGURÐARDÓTTIR
2009

URSULA BURNS
2009

HABEN GIRMA
2013

JANET MOCK
2014

SCHUYLER BAILAR
2016

JASILYN CHARGER
2016

MELATI AND ISABEL WIJSEN
2016

SHAMMA BINT SUHAIL FARIS MAZRUI
2016

A long time ago

THOMAS GALLAUDET
1817

SARAH WINNEMUCCA
1883

SUSAN LA FLESCHE
1889

SARAH BREEDLOVE
1906

PATSY MINK
1964

KATHARINE GRAHAM
1963

ED ROBERTS
1962

SIRIMAVO BANDARANAIKE
1960

GEORGE SHIMA
1913

LIN ZONGSU
1911

ERTHA PASCAL-TROUILLOT
1990

ÉDITH CRESSON
1991

ALTHEA GARRISON
1993

NELSON MANDELA
1994

KASHA NABAGESERA
2003

BARACK OBAMA
2009

ELLEN JOHNSON SIRLEAF
2005

ANGELA MERKEL
2005

OPRAH WINFREY
2003

SHIRIN EBADI
2003

MELINDA GATES
2017

HALIMA ADEN
2017

JACINDA ARDERN
2018

LEBRON JAMES
2018

MARVIA MALIK
2018

YARA SHAHIDI
2018

Time will tell!

111

FURTHER EXPLORATION

This book introduces you to some amazing people who did revolutionary things. Here are some additional reading and resources to help you learn more:

BOOKS

Belviso, Meg, and Pam Pollack. *Who Was Steve Jobs?* New York: Penguin Workshop, 2012.

Blumenthal, Karen. *Steve Jobs: The Man Who Thought Different*. New York: Feiwel & Friends, 2012.

Bowen, Andy Russell, and Elaine Wadsworth. *A World of Knowing: A Story About Thomas Hopkins Gallaudet*. Minneapolis: Carolrhoda Books, 1995.

Bundles, A'Lelia. *All About Madam C.J. Walker*. Indianapolis: Blue River Press, 2018.

Carson, Diana Pastora, and Patrick Wm. Connally. *Ed Roberts: Father of Disability Rights*. Indianapolis: Dog Ear Publishing, 2013.

Dunham, Montrew, and Meryl Henderson. *Thurgood Marshall: Young Justice*. New York: Aladdin Paperbacks, 1998.

Girma, Haben. *Haben: The Deafblind Woman Who Conquered Harvard Law*. New York: Twelve, 2019.

Henzel, Cynthia Kennedy. *Jacinda Ardern: Prime Minister of New Zealand*. Lake Elmo, Minnesota: Focus Readers, 2019.

Hughes, Libby. *Benazir Bhutto: From Prison to Prime Minister*. IUniverse, 2000.

Louie, Ai-Ling. *Patsy Mink, Mother of Title 9*. Bethesda, Maryland: Dragoneagle Press, 2018.

Menon, Sreelata. *Indira Gandhi: Child of Politics*. New York: Puffin, 2013.

Mock, Janet. *Redefining Realness: My Path to Womanhood, Identity, Love & So Much More*. New York: Atria Books, 2014.

Moss, Caroline, and Sinem Erkas. *Oprah Winfrey: Run the Show Like CEO*. Minneapolis: Frances Lincoln Children's Books, 2019.

Obama, Barack, and Loren Long. *Of Thee I Sing: A Letter to My Daughters*. New York: Puffin, 2018.

Ray, Deborah Kogan. *Paiute Princess: The Story of Sarah Winnemucca*. New York: Frances Foster Books, Farrar Straus Giroux, 2012.

Thomas, Garen. *Yes We Can: A Biography of President Barack Obama*. New York: Feiwel & Friends, 2008.

Wetzel, Dan. *Epic Athletes: LeBron James*. New York: Henry Holt, 2019.

Wezithombe, Umlando. *Nelson Mandela: The Authorized Comic Book*. New York: W.W. Norton & Co., 2009.

Yoo, Paula, and Jamel Akib. *Twenty-two Cents: Muhammad Yunus and the Village Bank*. New York: Lee & Low Books, 2014.

WEBSITES

Bill & Melinda Gates Foundation: https://www.gatesfoundation.org/en/

Time Magazine's Firsts: Women Who Are Changing the World: http://time.com/collection/firsts/

DOCUMENTARIES

Ellard, Melissa R., dir. *Nelson Mandela*, 2017.

Lesiak, Christine, and Princella P. RedCorn, dir. *Medicine Woman*, 2016.

Rice, Amy, and Alicia Sams, dir. *By the People: The Election of Barack Obama*, 2009.

ALEX HART is the pseudonym for a children's book editor and author who is the first person in his family to write and publish a book. He lives with his husband in Brooklyn, New York, and Hillsdale, New York.

JAY LESLIE is the first person in her family to become an author instead of a doctor. She graduated from Duke University with degrees in English, international comparative studies, and religion. Jay lives in Berlin, Germany, where she spends her time writing novels, learning new languages, and back-packing through the Black Forest. *Who Did It First? 50 Politicians, Activists, and Entrepreneurs Who Revolutionized the World* is her first book for children.

JAY-LESLIE.COM

NNEKA MYERS paints worlds filled with color, texture, life, and diversity. Based in Toronto, Ontario, she is the first in her family to become a full-time character designer and illustrator. Nneka can often be found looking for inspiration in vintage fashion, drinking tea with friends, or playing video games. *Who Did It First? 50 Politicians, Activists, and Entrepreneurs Who Revolutionized the World* is her first nonfiction book for children.

NNEKAMYERS.COM